Hurt 2 Heart

5 positive ways to win over the word in-law

Ayshna Mukherjee

Ukiyoto Publishing

Pal Pal Dil Ke Paas…

Dedication

First of all I will want to thank Ukiyoto for providing such a wonderful platform from where if I can make a mark, and then there will be no looking back. This, I believe will be the same thought for all other fellow authors sharing this wonderful platform. My best wishes to all of them! About the book that I have written, it is from my own true life experiences. Through this book I would want to pay homage/tribute to my Lt. Mother-in-law. She has been an enormous pillar of strength & hope even in the most trying times.It was she who has taught me to "Keep Going"!She herself has been a fighter all through her 85 years of life, and though life has been tough with her, she never gave up. Until the last 15 days when the Cancer insider her was ravaging her body. I have here showcased problems that I have faced with my mother-in-law and also tried to give solutions to them as well. It is all a matter of priority. The way you think. Just a little bit of tactfulness and Love, Trust & Respect for each other will see one through any storm. No relationship in this world can survive on its own. It is has to be a 2-way connect. This will not only help strengthen the mutual bonding but also prevent any big mistake from happening. It takes a hasty, rash decision to end any relationship, but years of effort to build the same. So why break it so easily? Why even give a chance to negativity? After all Life is one, and it deserves to be lived at the fullest!!! Hence leading an individual from the Hurt 2 Heart!!!

Preface

From Me 2 You!

Welcome to my book! Now all of you must be thinking who is this newbie out here? Out with so much of Gyan! Yes, Gyan it is. But I have tried my hands to accumulate all this so-called Gyan from my own life & experiences. Not much of my life, just halfway to Fifty, this thought of writing kept peeping out from its dark, not so sure nooks & corners. Mind says write, head says wait. Finally, with all the courage that I could muster here, I am writing out to all of out there. Hear me out!!!

I am Ayshna Mukherjee. Born & brought up with a middle-class upbringing with my parents visualizing me as a "Teacher". The safest option I believe. But Destiny had other plans chalked out. First, my name; Ayshna, was given to me with oodles of love by my maternal aunt. Which etymologically means curious to know new things. Lo! Behold! That is exactly what I am. Questions, questions, and more questions. Right from my childhood. Always tried to swim against the tide. Finally landed my anchor here in my present life. Not that I had a very happening life, but yes satisfactory. The ebb & flow of the wave of life has placed me on many uncertain shores where the beaches sometimes were very rocky and at other times full of quicksand.

Presently I am residing in Kolkata, famously known as the "City of Joy". It is also hailed as the Cultural Capital of India. The family comprises of my husband, my mother & me. It also had another member whom we have lost nearly two years back after a tough fight with Cancer. She is my Mother-in-law. And this accumulated Gyan that I am writing here is all because of her & the innumerable incidents which cross my mind. We shared an amazing bonding. Such that given a choice, I will always choose the memories that I have with her. Guess what! We connected wonderfully! The Connect was essential for both of us. It happened as well. Contributions from both ends and also from my husband. Not to forget that. Which my friend is vital in relationships these days. I will also want to say a big thank you to my mother, as she was the person who coaxed me out of my deep slumber amidst the first lockdown to start writing again. I was a bit shocked! Me & writing? After all these years. I had a habit of writing during my college and University days. She was aware of that. And that my friends was the beginning of this journey.

So here I am, penning or typing down Hurt 2 Heart! Why such a name? My life has been a journey of the same. Which I believe everybody does in their sphere. But choosing this title had an inner secret that I have never shared with anyone else till date. I have a deep respect for relationships. Be it any form. I have lost many and gained many as well. But we are not always able to connect with all of them. Not that they deserve any less, but the connection just does not happen. This is exactly why I have come out of my cocoon and decided to share with all of you the best connection I had ever made.That of my Bonding with Ma.My late Mother-in-law.And it is our story here that I am letting all of you have a glimpse of. This is such a relationship that is always in the line of fire. Very fragile & delicate if not handled properly. Everything about any family revolves around this.

In Part-I of my book, I have tried to take all of you back to your school days when life was so simple yet mesmerizing. Connect with me on that level, sit back and reminiscence about the golden days and let your mind roam free. Sit back, close your eyes, take a deep breath and connect with yourself-the inner you! Listen. There is so much waiting to be heard. Next, I have tried to make you mentally aware of the power of thoughts within you. Very important yet mundane things. From Connect, I take you to Think, and then you will find me slowly unveiling my story.

In Part-II of my book I have tried to bring out five different yet interlinked easy solutions so that this delicate chemistry between a mother-in-law and a daughter-in-law can be nurtured. This I will say is not only meant for would-be brides or grooms but also for people who are already married as well. Whatever pathways I have written here may or may not be applicable for all but even if a bit of it helps to improve this very important part of any family, please do try it out. If I am a woman who has achieved so much success, then it is my staunch belief that all of you who are reading this can definitely see and experience the same as well. Good Luck!!!!

CONTENTS

Part 1 - Connections…

Dusty Memoirs...

Lockdown# So much to do# Walk down Memory Lane# Way back to your Childhood!!! Let's Go...

The school takes you back to the lunch break past the fully-bloomed pale pink flowers of the bogunvillia to the partly opened school gate-What for??? An extra helping of " Hojmi" that extra bit of " Alu Kabli". Wow! Amazing! Awesome old days without much to do and it is actually "Food for Thought'!

Back home you come, you just have enough time to grab a meal & out you go to the open playground. Time then fleets by until you hear your neighboring Uncle/Aunty sternly asking you to go back home as it is nearing dusk. They were as good as your parents. They had the right too. No one would question them on the same. So many relations have faded out; some have even crossed the barrier of this mortal world. Hence in this lockdown, open your minds. Stop, Breathe & Re-Live your past from its dusty quarters. Reminiscence in the memories of people who are no more. There is still time. Connect. Just a call away.

Born a staunch Bengali, Durga Pujo has been an indispensable part of the growing-up years. Especially in your adolescent years, your father purchases the best sari for his Princess. Your mother drools over you and helps you to wear the sari & shows you the path to looking good. You proudly flaunt yourself in the new sari and sit in the pandal gossiping with like-minded friends belonging to the same locality. In this lockdown, make your spouse, children a part of these umpteen stories. Listen to your heart- if it yearns for just dial the number of such a long-lost friend & the rest they say is: "History repeats itself".

Now let us come back to the present- Life is all about the hustle & bustle. Things to do & Things not to do. Phew! Take a break in this lockdown. Stop in your tracks. Cultivate the 3R's. Relax, Rejuvenate

& Re-Live. As a couple just interchange your roles. Do small things for each other. Like preparing tea (mind you. Prepare it, don't make it). Prepare it with oodles of love, warmth & the very sense of belongingness to one another. Cut off the mobile, the laptop, the daily grind, sit together in a comfortable corner of your home & enjoy your evening tea with the years of your togetherness. Trust me it tastes Absolute Bliss!!! . Try it.

As parents, when was the last time did you set for a close chat with your child's friends? Ask yourself. Be honest. Forgo the past & open up to your children. Make family dinners a special experience with everyone participating in any topic available. Be their friend, not a parent. Open the flood gates of thoughts, respect theirs, & more still connect with them. Mix with their peer group. Share your golden days with them and see the magic unfold in front of you!!!.

Children should also take up the same ownership as their parents. Of bridging the gap between them & their parents. Spend time with them. Enjoy a lazy chat, have heated arguments. These are nothing but interactions amongst each other. It is lockdown; hence utilize it to the maximum.

Nature is healing itself. Heal with it. Indulge in it. Look up at the clear blue/ azure sky. Listen to the birds chirping. No pollution, no dirt & grease. No traffic jam. Mother Nature is nurturing her bruised self. Be a part of this healing touch! Let your soul heal.

In short, stay connected with yourself-your innermost YOU. Be alive & not just breathe. Let your conscience speak to you. We may never again get this chance. So connect with whoever, whatever, wherever is lost. Life is one- live it! As Gurudev Rabindranath Tagore says: "Where the mind is without fear & the head is held high. Into that country of freedom let my mind awake."Stay safe everyone!

Think-Tank...

Virtual days are back again! This time with a severe ferociousness, as if well-prepared from the last time. Still, do people have the time to sit back & think? Do they question themselves? Most likely not! The question keeps popping up in my mind: WHY? The ironic part is we all know the answer, but we pretend that we don't. Now that is extremely hypocritical. The mighty dragon named Corona has its deadly tentacles spread out everyone was. It is high time we take action. We need to manifest our deepest understanding of the very essence of Life. Life is incomplete without the acceptance of relationships. Where are we stranded? In front of Mother Nature...Tiny puny things. The problem is, we all know when and where we need to take action, but in our present state of mind, our ego does not let us. What will people say or think if we act differently? If we act with sympathy, compassion & empathy!! No way; it is not for us. This is the usual trend now.

No, I am not saying that we can't do anything. All that I am trying to convey is that all of us have been created as the Supreme Creation of the Almighty Power. We need to understand the whole meaning of the same. With this comes the onus of responsibility, the sense of logic, the sense of compassion, love, sensitivity, of fellow feeling. We are Human Beings--- Beings with a humane touch! Understand the hair-splitting difference between both. Feel it. That is what is required right now. Broaden your horizon, your outlook, and inculcate your fellow feelings towards one another. Trust me, try it! And see the magic unfolding in front of you!!! All of us are born magicians. There is nothing to learn. Just the need to delve deep and fathom your feelings. The problem lies exactly here. We are afraid to do so. What if, we see that our so-called nature of Dr. Jekyll is overshadowed by Mr.Hyde? We are afraid to see our dark, inner self. Or rather what lies beneath it? Maybe like a ship without a rudder and compass lost in the deep seas. Yes, the very question—What If?

This haunts us to no end. Just like an unknown, unseen warrior very similar to the virus presently wreaking havoc everywhere. Now that I have tried my hand at identifying the problem & the source of the same, it is time that we look towards the light, towards enlightenment.

The answer to all problems lies within us! Within the critical, sensitive human mind. Relationships are the same. Especially the one between a mother-in-law and that of her daughter-in-law. We just need to be training ourselves to look into the nook & corner of our minds. Into those places where thoughts confluence with each other. For that, we do not need anyone from outside to come & train us. Even if they do come, only a minor portion of the same can be identified. The rest lies upon each one of us! One of the best ways which I believe can work like magic is:

<u>Listening to people</u>. People now need to be heard. They need to vent out. And more so, they need a place where they can share their grief, their sorrow, their pain, their anxiety, their frustration without thinking twice. When a person is happy and has all positive things surrounding those people will be there for them, applauding them. But when one is lonely, when one needs to shed a tear or two—let them. Protect their privacy! You being a would-be daughter-in-law or a would-be mother-in-law feel that you are there for her & vice-versa. It is all about the feelings which come directly from the heart. Who knows that in the way, people might have been hurt, bled, and wounded? In this virtual world, this is the least that we can do for each other. Provided we have the mind too. Who knows that one day even you may be in the other person's shoes!!! What then? How do you feel? So, do broaden your horizons. Open up to people. Let people feel free & relaxed talking to you! It heals!!! Just like these lockdowns which heals the bruises made by the virus.

<u>Be Compassionate</u>! The big word right! Yes, it is! The mind becomes big; it learns to accumulate a lot of feelings, pathos, emotions, sympathy, and empathy as well. Learn to give, whatsoever it may be. Yes, one needs to be cautious. But one needs to be able to judge properly. Please do not judge a relationship based on certain set parameters. They may have existed ages or generations before but the world has changed and is ever-changing. Change in any form I believe is the only constant thing. This applies to both mother and daughter-in-law. There is no hard and fast rule for any relationship to succeed. Rather it lies on the shoulders of both the people within that relation. The next thing that I will suggest will be:

<u>Give Empathy, not sympathy</u>: In today's trying times, the best thing that will work is when you show empathy to people. Make people realize that you understand their difficulties. Work hard on trying to build trust. As I strongly believe when everything else fails, it is trust in a relationship that is so delicate that is the cementing force between the two involved in it. Try to indulge in small things for each other but do it without any expectation. Then see the wonders! I have done it myself. Trust my word; it works. Takes time, I agree. Let it. Nothing in this world happens all of a sudden. You need to invest time & energy into it. This should come from both ends. Whatever you do, do it from your heart. Your soul should be in complete support of you. Hypocrisy is like a weed growing in the garden of relations. Stay away from it. Instead, nurture the newly-grown sapling and see it grow to give you shade and a cool breeze when you may need it the most. Open your hearts to each other. Share your fears. Later see those very same fears gone with the wind. Leaving back a trail of laughter, joy & quick banter. Let them open their hearts to you. Once you can achieve that, what else will you need?

<u>Indulge in Story-Telling</u>: Get close to each other by sharing your personal stories of your survival fight, how you have faced the hardest of circumstances & still kept going. That will be your own Hurt 2 Heart story. It Inspires, encourages, and it builds Hope! It makes each of you come closer & accept you as their own. That is exactly what I have tried to share with all of you here. I have indulged in story-telling, a story of how by following certain very small paths ways one can reach and even maintain a wonderful relationship with each other. It can be from the mother-in-law's side or the daughter-in-law's side as well. Stories will differ from one another. But by wanting to listen to them you will also get a fair idea of the type of person you are living with. What she expects of you or rather from you! This will act as a lifeline and help you in your very own hot-seats of relations. What else do you need? The so-called battle is nearly won!!! Cheers to Happiness. Enjoy and bask in each other's company!!!!

Ode To A Fighter.....

People say that the relationship between a mother-in-law and a daughter-in-law is always on tenterhooks. It has to be handled tactfully with full practical wisdom. But lucky me. Not in my case. For me, it was only a term that was used for the sake of rhetoric. The word: IN-LAW!!! This was a common factor between me & my late Mother-in-law. I use the word 'Late' as she left this mortal world on the 3rd of December 2019.

Amidst this lockdown, when I have made my mind to pen down my thoughts in respect to my experiences in life, I have to mention "Ma". Let me give you, my readers a brief introduction about HER. She was a woman who was a fighter. In all respects & aspects of her life. She was an indomitable spirited person who never learned to give up. Except in her last 15 days when she could not anymore. She was a teacher for 40 long years. Singlehandedly she carried on her duties of a wife, mother, homemaker, daughter, daughter-in-law, and teacher. So many roles all spun into one thread of her 85 years.

I came into her life or rather she came into my life 6 years ago from today, way back in 2014. I still clearly remember the first time I spoke to her- I was nervous. But all thanks to my husband who had already prepared me to face her. Slowly I got accustomed to her speaking slowly, and incidentally, she started waiting for my call at some time of the day. She never expected much! Just one phone call in the whole day was enough for her. Funnily, I too started to see the watch and fixed a certain time in between office to make the call to her. Little did I realize then, what a connection we were building up.

I finally got to meet her for the very first time. A frail, dark-skinned emancipated old lady. The first visit officially before I became her " Daughter-in-law" immediately made me feel at ease. The nervousness had long bid Adieu. In its place warmth had stealthily made its way. We both basked in it. We never realized when Love for each other had crept in. Marriage happened, and with it came moving away from her physically to another city where my husband was working. She would not leave her Kolkata behind. But the connection was already made. I finally coaxed her into coming & sharing home space with us. Away from her Kolkata. She was not well at all. The 4th stage of Breast Cancer was eating her up from inside. Adding fuel to the fire were 3 Cerebral Strokes, leaving her with speech disorientation that never restored to normalcy. Hospital visits were a common thing for us. With time, she started depending on me wholly & solely. Whatever happened, I had to be beside her. Only then would she oblige the medical practitioners to attend to her.

Often she would be in pain, all the tests, medication, would exhaust her. I still vividly recall whenever we used to go to meet her during the visiting hours, she had two prioritized itineraries which I had to attend to. One how we were doing at home & second to bring her back home. The home was Heaven to her because of our presence. Let me admit very candidly, I used to be frustrated very often, feel like I had enough of everything. But despite everything I used to end up looking after her. The shiny, dazzling & sometimes mischievous smile on her dark, wrinkled, tired face did wonders. I can still feel her smile. It was so infectious!

Physically, she was withering away, but mentally she was like that "Last Leaf" in O'Henry's short story. As I now sit & write about her, so many thoughts crisscross my mind. She was a warrior, with an indomitable spirit. She was by nature like a Coconut-strong outside and pulpy soft inside. And immensely sweet to people who were very close to her. In her long 85 years, life has thrown loads of challenges to her, some of which succeeded in breaking her, but that was only temporary. She took her time but returned to normalcy. Her honesty, truthfulness, her broad-mindedness to name a few.

There are still many points to write about her. But why I am writing about her today is because in today's grim situation in this lockdown, when all of us are very insecure about what is going to happen, when will we return to normalcy, I thought of remembering her for her determination & will to fight it out. My husband & myself consider ourselves to be extremely lucky that we could be directly associated with her till she breathed her last. Her journey of Life had different shades, most of them were of a struggle, but that did not stop her. Instead, she kept flowing against the tide and finally reached shore safely.

I being her Daughter-in-law am blessed to have connected with such a lady. Incidentally, I lost my father to Lung Cancer as well, but then I could not look after him due to personal reasons. I always had guilt in my mind, about this and I believe that God has been kind to give me this chance to look after her. Times are very hard now, but we have to keep it going. We can't afford to lose our patience, determination, and our fighting spirit. This I wish for everyone because Life is one- We have to Love to Live it!!!!

CHEERS!!!!

Part 2

Path To Connect...

Connections have been established. Feelings have been stirred. Thought-process has been activated. Different dots demanding attention. Let's give that! Let us together dive into this journey and create a unique path that will lead us from the Hurt 2 the Heart! Yes, this is how I justify my book title.

For us, as a person born & brought up in India Marriage has always been celebrated as a complete Institution in itself. A union not only of the bride and the groom but of two completely different families, having nearly everything different from each other. We all are aware of this. But why do I need to mention this here? I know it may seem irritating to some. But there is a reason. Let me now divulge the secret to you by Readers. Through my book, I have tried my best to showcase from my own life & experiences how to create a very unique bond between a Mother-in-law & a Daughter-in-law. Which I have been immensely lucky to have experienced. Before I take all of you on this journey of mine, let me tell you that this book and its contents are not only meant for the mother-in-law or the daughter-in-law but also for the man of the house who is the would-be husband along with the father-in-law as well. It is only when these four wheels of the car called " Marriage" runs smoothly will that marriage be the strongest in the worst of storms and will be the support system of each other. A true family in the truest sense.

Now let me tell you my part of the story. I have been extremely fortunate & blessed to have been part of a wonderful relationship bonding with my late mother-in-law. I have mentioned quite many instances about that in Part-I of this book. Post her demise and during this entire phase of Corona impacting the whole world, I have deeply felt that I should be paying my respects to her by sharing our story with the world. I do not know but I feel that someone some were may need this healing touch. Mine has been a 2nd marriage for both of us. My husband & myself. We both had tasted bitterness had taken a very conscious decision to settle down for the rest of our lives with each other. And with that decision came to picture my Mother-in-law. My father-in-law had expired long back so it was a family of just 3 people. I confess that initially there had been hiccups between us but later on it had blossomed into such a beautiful flower whose essence I can still feel even after 2 years of her demise. Such my dear friends such is the power of relationships. For your convenience and connect my dear friends I am hereby enlisting some of the paths ways that I have tread upon to reach my goal.

1.   **The Ice-Breaker**: This dear reader is very important. Whatever you do, make sure that it should come from your heart. You are anticipating meeting the woman for whom today you have got the man in your life. She is his Mother. So, take a deep breath and Relax. It's perfectly ok to be nervous, but guess what the funny part is you are not the only one feeling nervous. People on the other side have the same feeling as well. So basically, it is a win-win situation. Trust me it is always better than you can physically meet her in person but like my case I had to speak to her over the phone, it was difficult. I stammered, I desperately wanted to drink water, and after some very normal talk was at a loss as to what to say next. Silence on both ends. An ominous one too! But for me, she popped up the next question all about my job way back then when we got married. Ah! Thank God! What a relief! My known area. Post that conversation, slowly we started interacting regularly so that acted as an ice-breaker. Let me explain this to all of you through an example. It has occurred to me. I still vividly remember the first day when I went to meet her before marriage. My husband accompanied me and all along he tried his best to reassure me that all would go well. But I was apprehensive, you can understand the feeling. She opened the door with a smile. I bent down and touched her feet which are the normal culture in Bengal. We went in and settled down and I could feel that she was observing me. It made me very uncomfortable at first. But slowly as we kept talking and she asked me about my office, the work that I do I relaxed. But was still tensed. She then got up to go to the kitchen to prepare tea for all of us. Suddenly as if on cue, I blurted out that I be allowed to prepare tea for the three of us. To which she surprisingly obliged. We went to the kitchen together and she showed me where all the ingredients were stored. I asked her preference of what type of tea would

she prefer to have. The answer was:" Whichever you like". Tea was made, and then when I started to talk with her I somewhat felt much more relaxed. I took her to leave for that day. Now when I asked her as to whether the tea was made properly or not, she said: "What matters is that you made it". Taste is something which is not the important thing. Now, my friends, this is what I say acted as an Ice-Breaker. It first came from her end. She in her small way tried to make me comfortable. But wait there is more to add to this story. We met again after a few days and this time she insisted that I have lunch with both of them. I obliged. Not knowing what was in store for me. I helped her lay the table, and then all of us sat down to eat. The next moment something very unusual happened. She insisted that she feed me and made little balls of rice & fish curry that she had prepared and fed me with her own hands. I did not know how to react. I was stunned. That is why I say that one should always have the heart to bridge the gap if at all it is a gap. Now I leave it to you my readers to ponder that how could I not connect with such a lady? Was I left with any other choice? I believe your answer will be a big NO. Exactly so.

2.   **<u>Role of a Mediator</u>:** Now a word of caution my dear readers, choose your life partner wisely. He has to enact the role of a mediator between the both of you. This pointer goes out not only to all my would-be groom readers but also to men who are already married; you too have a great deal of responsibility on your shoulders. Not everyone may agree to this but there is no harm in slightly broadening your horizon and acting as a solid anchor to both the important ladies in your life. Every man has this dilemma in life: To interfere or not to interfere. An eternal Hamletian problem. But the answer lies hidden to all. You actually will not need to interfere at all. Just be a good mediator in the initial stages and the rest will fall in place. An example from my own life will throw light on the same. When my husband & myself took a unanimous decision to get married, the best surprise to me was when he one day told me that he wanted to talk to me about his mother. Very patiently, with the utmost care, he explained about his mother and her very nature. Not only did he mention her wonderful qualities as a person but also showed me the shortcomings that were within her. Adding along with that that all of us have shortcomings. We are human beings. So it is perfectly ok. Along with that he also suggested a few tricks that would help me to deal with her shortcomings

post marriage. This friend is a mammoth task. Not everyone will be able to support this. But my humble request to all men out there, do think it over and if that applies to you and your family, just do it. I am pretty much aware that it is not an easy thing to digest. But my own experience showcases that it works. So when I stepped into the house officially as the daughter-in-law, I knew exactly how to react in different situations. In my case, I will want to say a huge Thank you to my husband for supporting me & standing by me whenever required. But by saying this I never say that you disrespect your mother. No Never. But one I am trying to convey is that do not be blind to her shortcomings. If there is a necessary step into the scene and speak to each one differently. But a word of caution. Never do the blunder of complaining against one in front of another. That my friends will be a "Himalayan Blunder". You remain stern where ever required and if the need arises to speak to each other about their differences separately. This I say is exactly what my husband did. Both my mother-in-law and I had our fair share of differences. Of opinion. My husband gave a patient hearing to each of us. Then whoever was correct stood by her and spoke to the other lady explaining why she was not wrong, but incorrect. He was never biased about his mother or me. He had the guts to call a Spade a spade! Think about this aspect. Once this was sorted, things were back to normalcy once again. I love him for this frank demeanor. Initially, it may sound crazy, I may sound to be biased but if this can be done then both the delicate relations can be handled by both the ladies in your lives at ease. Now give it a thought and do try it out. And see the magic unfold in front of you. To all the wonderful men out there, if you have the courage just go for it. You will no longer have to feel squeezed between the two ladies post–marriage as by then they will be so much used to each other that you will just become a mute spectator. Enjoy being so!

3.   **<u>Respect her feelings</u>**: She is a person who is your husband's mother. She is a lady who is equivalent to your mother. Think how you would feel if someone would have shown disrespect to your mother. Just the same here. Treat her with the utmost respect. Never do it just for the heck of doing the same. It should come from your inner self. Show respect to her family, her thoughts, her ideologies, her beliefs, her traditions which she has maintained over the years. There will be some of which you will not be able to accept. Point

taken. But let me ask you one question? Do you land up with any better option? Never do nag or complain to your husband or father-in-law about this. That will only add fuel to the fire. Instead, sit and communicate with your mother-in-law and ask her to guide you in everything you do. She will. This will make her feel more senior, more secure with you. She will not consider you to be a deterrent to her family. What did I do? Exactly what I am asking all of you to do. By doing this, your position does not get weak instead you slowly but surely move to a reliable place in her heart. That is one of the ways or paths that will lead from Hurt 2 Heart! A connection will be built for a lifetime. To put it more simply. She is a senior person and it will not hurt us to show respect for an aged person. After all, this is a life cycle that is bound to change one day. Try it out. From the heart. That is the best way to win a person to you. Just let me share a story here as well. As I have already mentioned that my Father-in-law had expired long back. So each year on his death Anniversary I always made it a point to decorate his picture and my husband would bring sweets and I used to offer my respects to him. Ma never told me to do anything extra or anything special for that day. But from the time I came to know about the date, I did the above. She never said anything but her eyes did. And that meant the world to me. I could read her contentment that I was remembering her husband and doing my bit. That was enough for her. Very ironically, she did not remember her birthday, the way it is with elderly people. We all know that. I with the help and support from my husband have tried to do my bit. Arrange for a cake, a chocolate one as she loved the flavor. Either I cooked all the food items she liked or asked our cook too so. Once till the time she was able to venture out, we celebrated her birthday at a famous hotel. She was overwhelmed and was nearly in tears when she saw the arrangements made only for her. For her, someone could do this much even was such a huge thing. Even when we celebrated her birthday simply at home and asked her to cut the cake and gave her cream or chocolate facial she giggled with laughter while her eyes remained moist. In this context, let me tell you that once the cake was cut and offered to her she would finish it in no seconds. Just like a five-year-old. As if the cake had wings and would fly off far away from her!!! That was Ma. So many more incidents to share. But my main purpose is to let all of you have a feeling that if you want to do something for someone just do it. Please follow your heart. Listen to what it says and act accordingly. I can bet on this that you will see yourself in a better situation and a better understanding of each other.

4.   **<u>Show Affection</u>:** Even if you may not like it always try to be affectionate towards her. You do not have to do mammoth tasks for that. Just sitting and chatting with her, having tea or coffee with her, watching TV with her, listening to different stories she has to tell you, wanting to learn about your spouse and his choices while he grew up. Ask her to share her own life story. Now if you are in a dilemma on how to tackle her just ask her to share her story and how she used to deal with her mother-in-law and you will get your answers. Sometimes sweetly reviewing things helps solve a lot of questions. Give her your time. Keep the communication going. Even though it may be related to trivial matters. Let her make decisions. You may not like them but never raise your voice. Instead later when you find a suitable time & place give her your suggestion in a subtle manner. Make sure that it has logic and then give a suggestion to her about trying and implementing it in the future. Only if she thinks it to be suitable. Let the ball be in her court. For my part, my mother-in-law had left all major decisions in my hand. But despite that, I made it a point always to inform her so ever I was doing. In my case, she was not well and one fine day she walked up to me and handed over her almirah keys to me saying that now I should be handling everything henceforth. I was stunned as this was something unexpected for her. But then I was convinced that with due time I had been able to gain her trust and confidence. I took the keys but kept it under her pillows saying that whenever I would need anything I would take it from her after informing her. This I maintained till her demise. Try doing this and magic is bound to happen. After all, she is also a human being. We must oblige her with the same. Other than this I will share another story here. My husband and I had always made it a point that every day in the morning we used to have our morning tea together along with Ma in her room. This was a very special time that we shared with her and which we miss very much now. She never said that she wanted our company, but her eyes

would always be shining with a streak of joy. On the days when she would be in the hospital, she would always fidget to come back home to her room & her bed at the earliest. Mention must also be made of another incident. Other than this morning tea we would have our evening tea & watch daily Bengali soap operas with her. Since she was physically pretty unwell, & had restrictions on the movement she used to stay at home most of the time in her room. Hence we had taken this very conscious decision to spend time with her. Try this out my friends or at least something like this which is suitable for your family and then see the difference! Trust me the internal, invisible bond that is there within each family will grow & nurture with time. All this will have a positive effect on the next generation as well. Strong family values will be installed in them from a very tender age which is of utmost necessity in today's world. Here's wishing all of you out there: "All the very best"!

5.   **<u>Shower your love</u>**: Whatever relationships we share on this earth our first moral duty toward fellow human beings is to be Human! All people deserve to be loved and respected. And when it comes to the person being your husband's mother, it is all the more necessary. Now a lot of you will say not everyone is the same. Absolutely! Not everyone will be the same. But my question is? For a handful of people who are not positive-minded, why should we neglect the positive-minded people? People whom we cannot change, we have to accept them the way they are. But people who give each other the space to change should also reciprocate in the same way. In my case, as I have mentioned earlier that Ma was not well and always had to be taken to hospitals and different medical fraternities for nearly 4 years. Those were hard times for all the three of us. The regular visit to the doctors was making life pretty challenging. With each passing day, Ma was becoming more and more completely dependent on me. To the extent that I had to accompany her to her tests and her doctors and only then in my presence would she allow the medical fraternity to do their job! The strain & pressure were taking their toll on us, but she was so strong. She was weak, yes, but her spirits were ever flying high! That my dear readers are all the love that she showered on both of us, especially me. And I was blessed!

That was the way it was with both of us. Just pure, simple love we had & felt for each other. There came a time when she depended on me more than her son. Lucky me! But yes that happened. Now that I am writing this down, she must be watching over me from her heavenly abode and smiling her infectious smile!!! Love as they say knows no bounds. I too in my ways tried my level best to shower her with all the love that could be possible is. She never demanded anything but somehow by God's grace I could understand what she did not say. I should mention here that she had suffered from four cerebral strokes and her speech became quite disoriented. So we had by staying very close to her developed that understanding. Love, I believe that what I had received from her had made this possible. She was a small eater. But loved having sweets in any form or shape. Especially the dessert which we call "Chutni" made of tomatoes, raisins and cashew nuts. In fact, in her last two months till the time, she could have solid food she preferred to have rice mixed with this chutney. I always made it a point either to cook it myself or ask our cook to prepare it for her. No, never did she ask me or force me to prepare it for her. I just knew it. I understood. No questions asked. Not required. She also loved to have chocolates, so whenever we went out we always brought some chocolates, her favorite Hojmi, or even some small gifts for any festive occasion. During Durga Puja, when we came back home after doing shopping, one should have seen that mischievous glint in her eyes, and would immediately demand to see what purchases had been made. No, not for her clothes. She never asked for one. But to see what we had purchased for us. As I write this, I can visualize her that she used to force both me & my husband to wear it and show it to her then & there. She behaved like a small child who had just got her new toy. Where in the world can I ask for such unconditional love? Well my friends, just go and do it. Don't think too much. Let your hurt take you to your heart! Enjoy the ride.

So my dearest readers this is in short all I have to say about these five simple steps that have helped me to establish a wonderful and life-long relationship with my mother-in-law. There will be a lot many more points to be added and for that, I am inviting all of you to please take out time to read this book, give your valuable feedback. One thing that I can vouch for is bys following these five pointers in my life has helped me achieve this much in life, I am very sure that it will be helpful to all of you out there. Yes, for this relationship to click it is of utmost importance that there is a response from both ends. If it does, trust me then that family will be termed an ideal family residing in peace with one another. So my dear readers I will wrap up my book and leave all of you with this thought: "Zindagi ek safar hain suhana, yahan kaal kya ho kisne jana"!!! Enjoy life, Live, Laugh & Love!!!

Cheers!!! ☺☺☺

About the Author

Ayshna Mukherjee

Ayshna Mukherjee was born in a small town by the name Chandannagar, which is part of the Hooghly District in West Bengal. Ayshna, has completed her Masters in English Language & Literature from the University of Burdwan & has ventured out on her first book. She is an ardent lover of nature. Especially the mountains haunt her and beacon her to go to them. She presently resides in Kolkata along with her Husband who is a Financial Consultant by profession. Other than this, she is actively involved with an NGO which provides free education to Underprivileged children. She also has a very soft corner for both cats & dogs. She has plans to do something for them in the future. This book is very close to her heart and is closely intertwined with her passion for expressing herself through her writings. She completely believes in the saying that "The pen is mightier than the sword"! Her mantra for life is: And Miles to go before I sleep,

And Miles to go before I sleep!

Hope to see the next venture from her shortly as she has nearly decided on her next topic. We wish her the very best!! She is reachable @: *ayshnamukherjee@gmail.com.*